The Lord is My Shepherd

from Psalm 23

Ingrid Beck

Westminster John Knox Press
Louisville, Kentucky

Psalm 23
A Psalm of David

The Lord is my Shepherd;

I have everything I need.

He makes me lie down in green pastures;

He leads me beside quiet waters.

He restores my soul;

He leads me on paths that are right for
his name's sake.

Even though I walk through the valley of the shadow of death,
I will fear no evil; for you are with me.
Your rod and your staff, they comfort me.

You prepare a table before me in the presence of my enemies.
You anoint my head with oil;
My cup overflows.
Surely goodness and mercy will follow me all the days of my life;
and I will dwell in the house of the Lord forever.

The Lord looks after me.

*H*e makes sure I have everything I need.

*H*e gives me green grass to lie down in,

And quiet waters to enjoy.

*H*e makes me feel so good,

$\mathcal{A}$nd he tells me the right things to do.

$\mathcal{E}$ven though I may be in frightening situations, I never need to be scared, for I know the Lord is always with me, although I cannot see him.

Our Father
who is in Heaven.
Hallowed be your name
Your kingdom come,
your Will be done,
on Earth, as it is
in Heaven.

He comforts me,

Give us today our daily bread, and forgive us our sins, as we forgive those who sin against us. Lead us not into temptation, but deliver us from evil, for the kingdom, the power, and the glory are yours forever and ever. Amen.

and looks after me.

*T*he Lord makes sure I have food to eat, and he keeps my enemies away from me.

*H*e blesses me.

And because he is so good,
I feel so happy inside.

*T*am sure goodness and love will
follow me all of my life.

And one day I shall go to live in
the Lord's house, forever.

Published in 1999 by Westminster John Knox Press, Louisville, Kentucky

Copyright© 1999 Hunt & Thorpe Text and Illustrations©1999 Ingrid Beck

First published in Great Britain under the title *The Lord is My Shepherd* by Hunt & Thorpe, Ropley, Hants

For information, address
Westminster John Knox Press, 100 Witherspoon Street, Louisville, Kentucky 40202-1396, USA.

Printed in Hong Kong/China
99 00 01 02 03 04 05 06 07 08 - 10 9 8 7 6 5 4 3 2 1

Based on the **Holy Bible**, **New International Version**, Hodder & Stoughton, 9th Edition, May 1991

Westminster John Knox Press
Louisville, Kentucky